chicken

chicken

This edition first published in the U.K. in 1999 by Hamlyn for WHSmith, Greenbridge Road, Swindon SN3 3LD

Copyright © 1999 Octopus Publishing Group Limited

Octopus Publishing Group Limited
2–4 Heron Quays
London E14 4JP

ISBN 0 600 59885 3
Printed in China

Notes

1 Standard level spoon measurements are used in all recipes.

1 tablespoon = one 15 ml spoon
1 teaspoon = one 5 ml spoon

2 Both imperial and metric measurements have been given in all recipes. Use one set of measurements only and not a mixture of both.

3 Measurements for canned food have been given as a standard metric measurement.

4 Eggs should be medium unless otherwise stated. The Department of Health advises that eggs should not be consumed raw. This book may contain dishes made with lightly cooked eggs. It is prudent for more vulnerable people, such as pregnant and nursing mothers, invalids, the elderly, babies and young children, to avoid uncooked or lightly cooked dishes made with eggs. Once prepared, these dishes should be used immediately.

5 Milk should be full fat unless otherwise stated.

6 Poultry should be cooked thoroughly. To test if poultry is cooked, pierce the flesh through the thickest part with a skewer or fork – the juices should run clear, never pink or red.

7 Fresh herbs should be used unless otherwise stated. If unavailable, use dried herbs as an alternative but halve the quantities stated.

8 Pepper should be freshly ground black pepper unless otherwise stated; season according to taste.

9 Ovens should be preheated to the specified temperature – if using a fan-assisted oven, follow the manufacturer's instructions for adjusting the time and the temperature.

10 Do not re-freeze a dish that has been frozen previously.

11 This book includes dishes made with nuts and nut derivatives. It is advisable for customers with known allergic reactions to nuts and nut derivatives and those who may be potentially vulnerable to these allergies, such as pregnant and nursing mothers, invalids, the elderly, babies and children, to avoid dishes made with nuts and nut oils. It is also prudent to check the labels of pre-prepared ingredients for the possible inclusion of nut derivatives.

12 Vegetarians should look for the 'V' symbol on a cheese to ensure it is made with vegetarian rennet. There are vegetarian forms of Parmesan, feta, Cheddar, Cheshire, red Leicester, dolcelatte and many goats' cheeses, among others.

contents

Chicken is one of the most popular of all savoury foods – quick, versatile and easy to cook – and suitable for both simple and sophisticated dishes, as this wide-ranging collection of recipes shows. It is also a favourite all over the world and chicken dishes can be found stamped with every national style and choice of flavourings.

The best chickens are free-range birds, but these are more expensive than battery chickens. Factory-farmed chicken comes in several varieties, including maize-fed or corn-fed chickens, which have creamy yellow flesh from the corn on which they are fed. The cheapest birds are those found in the freezer section of supermarkets. These do not have the flavour of fresh birds but are nutritious and useful for making stock.

Whole Chickens

These are usually labelled oven-ready, meaning that they have been plucked, drawn and trussed, and can weigh anything from 500 g (1 lb) for the smallest poussins, which make an individual serving, to huge 4 kg (8 lb) monsters, sometimes called capons, which can be served as an alternative to the Christmas turkey. Spring chickens, which are up to 12 weeks old and weigh 1.25 kg (2½ lb), will feed 2–3 people. When choosing a chicken, look for a bird with a plump white breast, smooth and pliable legs and moist but not wet skin which is free of dark patches and has not split. Whole chickens can be roasted, pot-roasted, poached, braised or steamed.

Chicken Pieces

Ready-jointed chicken is sold as quarters (including leg and breast meat, with bones in), breasts, thighs and drumsticks. Thighs and drumsticks are good for stews, casseroles and barbecuing. Breasts are available with and without bones and skin. The latter is sometimes labelled as fillet. All types of breast meat are top quality lean meat and cook very quickly. Use them for pan-frying, grilling, poaching, steaming, stir-frying and sautéing. Supermarket chickens are usually sold without their giblets, so if you want them for a recipe you will have to buy your chicken from a butcher. Chicken livers, on the other hand, are sold in tubs in the freezer section of supermarkets.

Chicken & Health

Raw poultry contains low levels of bacteria, including salmonella, which cause food poisoning, but correct storage and handling will render the bacteria harmless. When you get a fresh chicken home, remove the plastic

chef's salad ●

chicken & sweetcorn soup ●

chicken liver pâté ●

chilli chicken drumsticks ●

chicken & leek soup ●

honeyed chicken wings ●

chicken & raisin salad ●

chicken & ham filo parcels ●

marinated chicken kebabs ●

parmesan chicken drumsticks ●

steamed chicken dumplings ●

stir-fried lemon chicken with vegetables ●

club sandwich ●

smoked chicken & citrus salad ●

chicken & avocado salad ●

small
courses

chef's salad

1 First make the dressing. Put all the ingredients into a screwtop jar and shake vigorously until well combined.

2 Tear the lettuce into bite-sized pieces and place them in a large salad bowl with the mixed herb sprigs. Toss together lightly.

3 Add all the remaining ingredients, except the dressing, and salt and pepper to taste.

4 Just before serving, spoon over the dressing and toss lightly.

1 small lettuce (e.g. round, red oakleaf, batavia, frisé), separated into leaves

small handful of mixed herb sprigs

¼ cucumber, thinly sliced

25 g (1 oz) walnut pieces

about 250 g (8 oz) cooked chicken, diced

125 g (4 oz) smoked ham, cut into strips

75 g (3 oz) cheese (e.g. Edam, Emmental, mature Cheddar), crumbled

handful of seedless grapes, halved (optional)

salt and pepper

French Dressing:

2 tablespoons red or white wine vinegar

1–2 garlic cloves, crushed

2 teaspoons Dijon mustard

¼ teaspoon caster sugar

6 tablespoons olive oil

salt and pepper

Serves 4

Preparation time: 20 minutes

chicken & sweetcorn soup

1 Pour the stock into a large saucepan and add 250 g (8 oz) of the sweetcorn. Bring to the boil, add salt and pepper to taste, cover and simmer for 15 minutes.

2 Pour the soup into a food processor or blender and blend until smooth, then return it to the pan. Reheat the soup. If it is not thick enough for your liking, blend the cornflour with the water to make a thin paste, stir it into the soup and bring to the boil, stirring. Add the remaining sweetcorn and the reserved chopped chicken and simmer for 5 minutes.

3 Taste and adjust the seasoning before serving, and garnish with the red pepper dice and strips.

900 ml (1½ pints) Chicken Stock (see page 9), with a little of the cooked chicken reserved and chopped

375 g (12 oz) sweetcorn kernels

2 teaspoons cornflour (optional)

1 tablespoon water (optional)

salt and pepper

red pepper dice and strips, to garnish

Serves 4
Preparation time: 10 minutes
Cooking time: 20–25 minutes

1 Melt the butter in a large saucepan. Add the bacon, garlic and onion and cook gently for 3 minutes. Stir in the chicken livers and cook for 5 minutes. Season liberally with salt and pepper. Stir in the herbs and mushrooms. Add the sherry and cook until the liquid has evaporated. Leave to cool, then blend in a food processor or blender until smooth. Stir in the cream and the lemon juice.

2 Spoon the pâté into a greased ovenproof dish. Cover with a lid and stand the dish in a roasting tin filled with 2.5 cm (1 inch) water. Bake in a preheated oven, 150°C (300°F), Gas Mark 2, for 2–2½ hours, until cooked through. Leave to cool then cover and chill until required.

3 Garnish the pâté with watercress, and serve with hot toast or French bread.

125 g (4 oz) butter

250 g (8 oz) rindless back bacon, chopped

4 garlic cloves, crushed

2 small onions, chopped

1 kg (2 lb) chicken livers, chopped

4 thyme sprigs

4 parsley sprigs

250 g (8 oz) button mushrooms, chopped

125 ml (4 fl oz) dry sherry

125 ml (4 fl oz) double cream

2 teaspoons lemon juice

salt and pepper

watercress sprigs, to garnish

Serves 12	
Preparation time: 20 minutes	
Cooking time: 2–2½ hours	

chicken liver pâté

■ This pâté will keep well in the refrigerator for at least a week – and for several weeks if it is completely sealed with a layer of lard or clarified butter on top.

chilli chicken drumsticks

1 Heat the oil in a frying pan and fry the onion and garlic until soft and lightly coloured. Add the ketchup, Worcestershire sauce, chilli seasoning, vinegar, jam and mustard and bring slowly to the boil. Simmer gently for 2 minutes, then remove the pan from the heat and leave to cool.

2 Arrange the drumsticks in a shallow dish in a single layer and pour the sauce over them. Cover and leave to marinate in a cool place for at least 3 hours, turning the drumsticks occasionally.

3 Drain the marinade from the drumsticks and reserve. Put the drumsticks under a preheated moderate grill and cook for about 8–10 minutes on each side until they are cooked through and well browned. Put them on to a warmed platter and garnish with parsley sprigs.

4 Heat the reserved marinade in a saucepan and serve with the drumsticks.

2 tablespoons oil

1 onion, finely chopped

1 garlic clove, crushed

150 ml (¼ pint) tomato ketchup

3 tablespoons Worcestershire sauce

2–3 teaspoons chilli seasoning

150 ml (¼ pint) red wine vinegar

2–3 tablespoons apricot jam

1 teaspoon mustard powder

20 chicken drumsticks

parsley sprigs, to garnish

Serves 10

Preparation time: 20 minutes, plus marinating

Cooking time: about 20 minutes

1 Put the chicken into a large saucepan and add the lemon rind, onion, carrots and celery. Pour in the water to cover, then add the bouquet garni and salt and pepper to taste. Bring to the boil over a moderate heat. Lower the heat, cover and simmer for 1½ hours or until the chicken is tender and the juices run clear when the thickest part of a thigh is pierced with a fork.

2 Lift the chicken out of the liquid and leave until cool enough to handle. Remove and discard the lemon rind and bouquet garni.

3 Meanwhile, add the leeks to the liquid in the pan and simmer, uncovered, over a moderate heat for 10 minutes or until just tender. Remove the chicken meat from the bones, and discard all skin and fat. Cut the meat into bite-sized pieces.

4 Crumble the stock cubes in a bowl, add the egg yolk and cream and stir well to mix. Add a few spoonfuls of the hot soup liquid and stir well again, then whisk this mixture gradually back into the soup. Add the chicken and simmer over a gentle heat, stirring constantly, for about 5 minutes until the chicken is heated through and the soup has thickened slightly.

5 Remove the soup from the heat and stir in the lemon rind and parsley. Taste for seasoning and serve at once.

2 kg (4 lb) oven-ready chicken, giblets removed

thinly pared rind of 1 lemon

1 onion, thinly sliced

3 carrots, thinly sliced

2 celery sticks, thinly sliced

2–2.5 litres (3½–4 pints) water

1 large bouquet garni

3 leeks, trimmed, cleaned and thickly sliced

1–2 chicken stock cubes, according to taste (optional)

1 egg yolk

4 tablespoons double cream

salt and pepper

finely grated rind of 1 lemon

2 tablespoons finely chopped parsley

Serves 4–6	
Preparation time: 20 minutes	
Cooking time: about 1¾ hours	

chicken & leek soup

honeyed chicken wings

1 To make the marinade, mix together all the ingredients in a bowl, mixing thoroughly until combined. Put the chicken wings into a shallow bowl and pour over the marinade. Spread the marinade all over them, then cover and leave in a cool place for 2 hours.

2 Meanwhile, make the sauce. Heat the oil in a small saucepan and fry the onion for about 5 minutes until golden brown. Stir in the sugar, lime juice and peanut butter, and then add the creamed coconut, a little at a time. Add the salt and cook over a gentle heat until smooth and thick. Set aside.

3 Remove the chicken wings from the marinade and place them on a rack in a baking tray. Cook in a preheated oven, 190°C (375°F), Gas Mark 5, for 15–20 minutes, until golden brown and cooked through, basting from time to time with any remaining marinade. Alternatively, grill for 5–7 minutes on each side. Serve with the warm dipping sauce.

12 chicken wings, trimmed

Marinade:

3 tablespoons soy sauce

4 tablespoons clear honey

2 tablespoons vinegar

1 tablespoon sherry

2 teaspoons soft brown sugar

½ teaspoon ground ginger

1 garlic clove, crushed

Dipping Sauce:

2 tablespoons olive oil

2 tablespoons grated onion

2 tablespoons brown sugar

1 teaspoon lime juice

2 tablespoons peanut butter

6 tablespoons creamed coconut

pinch of salt

Serves 4

Preparation time: 15 minutes, plus marinating

Cooking time: 20–25 minutes

40 g (1½ oz) raisins

juice of 1 small orange

pinch of ground cloves

1 teaspoon olive oil

50 g (2 oz) blanched almonds, halved

500 g (1 lb) cooked chicken, cut into strips

1 head radicchio, shredded

1 little gem lettuce, shredded

1 tablespoon French dressing (see page 13)

salt and pepper

handful of parsley leaves, to garnish

1 Put the raisins, orange juice and ground cloves into a small saucepan. Heat until boiling then remove from the heat and leave to stand for about 30 minutes to plump the raisins.

2 Heat the oil in a small saucepan over a moderate heat and brown the almonds, stirring constantly until golden.

3 Put the raisins, almonds, chicken and shredded salad leaves into a serving bowl. Toss and season well with salt and pepper. To serve, spoon over the dressing and scatter with parsley leaves.

Serves 4

Preparation time: 15 minutes, plus standing

Cooking time: about 12 minutes

chicken & raisin salad

1   Split the chicken breasts almost in half horizontally, open them out and place them between two sheets of clingfilm. Beat with a rolling pin to flatten them. Arrange the chicken over a large sheet of foil, overlapping the pieces slightly to form a 20 x 25 cm (8 x 10 inch) rectangle. Cover evenly with the slices of ham.

2   Heat the oil in a saucepan, add the shallots and fry for about 5 minutes until softened. Remove from the heat and stir in the watercress, feta, lemon juice, egg and season with salt and pepper. Mix well. Spread the mixture evenly over the ham to within 1 cm (½ inch) of the edge. Using the foil to help you, roll up the chicken, ham and filling from one long end. Wrap the foil around the roll and set aside.

3   Mix together the melted butter and mustard. Layer 3 or 4 sheets of filo, depending on their thickness, on an oiled baking sheet, brushing each one thinly with mustard butter. Carefully unwrap the chicken roll from the foil and place it in the centre. Arrange 3 more sheets of filo pastry over the top, brushing each one lightly with mustard butter. Scrunch 2 sheets of filo and arrange over the top. Press round the edge to seal the filling, then brush the top with any remaining butter.

4   Bake in a preheated oven, 190°C (375°F), Gas Mark 5, for 45–50 minutes until the pastry is crisp and golden brown. Serve warm or cold, cut into thick slices.

750 g (1½ lb) boneless, skinless chicken breasts

250 g (8 oz) sliced cooked ham

1 tablespoon sunflower oil

2 shallots, finely chopped

125 g (4 oz) watercress, chopped

125 g (4 oz) feta cheese, crumbled

1 tablespoon lemon juice

1 egg, beaten

50 g (2 oz) butter, melted

2 teaspoons wholegrain mustard

275 g (9 oz) packet filo pastry

salt and pepper

Serves 8

Preparation time: 30 minutes

Cooking time: 45–50 minutes

chicken & ham filo parcels

marinated chicken kebabs

1 To make the marinade, squeeze the lime or lemon juice into a large bowl and add the honey, chopped chilli and olive oil and stir until the mixture is well blended and smooth. Add the chicken to the marinade and mix gently until well coated. Cover and chill for at least 1 hour.

2 Thread the chicken on to pre-soaked wooden skewers and brush with the marinade. Place under a preheated hot grill or cook over a barbecue for 15–20 minutes, turning occasionally, until the chicken is tender and golden brown. Brush the kebabs with more marinade if necessary.

3 Meanwhile, make the avocado sauce. Blend the olive oil and vinegar in a bowl then beat in the mashed avocado until thick and smooth. Stir in the chopped tomato and spring onions, and the soured cream. Serve the kebabs hot, with the avocado sauce and the pomegranate seeds.

6 boneless, skinless chicken breasts, cut into large chunks

seeds of 1 pomegranate, to serve

Marinade:

juice of 2 limes or lemons

1 tablespoon honey

1 green chilli, finely chopped

2 tablespoons olive oil

Avocado Sauce:

3 tablespoons olive oil

1 tablespoon red wine vinegar

1 large avocado, peeled, stoned and mashed

1 large tomato, skinned and chopped

2 spring onions, chopped

125 ml (4 fl oz) soured cream

Serves 4
Preparation time: 15 minutes, plus marinating
Cooking time: 15–20 minutes

1 Mix the breadcrumbs and Parmesan cheese in a bowl. Season the flour with salt and pepper and sprinkle on a plate. Put the eggs in another bowl.

2 Coat the drumsticks with the seasoned flour, shaking off any excess, then dip them in the egg and roll in the breadcrumbs. Arrange on a plate, cover and chill for 30 minutes.

3 Cook the drumsticks under a preheated grill for 15–20 minutes or until they are cooked through and the juices run clear when pierced with a fork. Serve hot or cold, garnished with rosemary sprigs.

50 g (2 oz) fresh white breadcrumbs

50 g (2 oz) Parmesan cheese, finely grated

2 tablespoons plain flour

2 eggs, beaten

8 large chicken drumsticks, skinned

salt and pepper

rosemary sprigs, to garnish

Serves 4

Preparation time: 15 minutes, plus chilling

Cooking time: 15–20 minutes

parmesan chicken drumsticks

steamed chicken dumplings

1 Sift the flour into a mixing bowl and pour in the water. Mix well to form a dough. Knead for 5 minutes then place in a bowl, cover with a damp cloth and leave for 10 minutes.

2 Meanwhile, make the filling. Cut the chicken into small pieces and place in a bowl with the bamboo shoots, spring onions, ginger, sugar, soy sauce, sherry, stock, oil and salt. Mix thoroughly.

3 Cut the dough in half and shape each piece into a long roll. Cut each roll into 16 slices, flatten them into rounds and roll out to make circles 7 cm (3 inches) in diameter. Put 1 tablespoon of filling in the centre of each circle, gather up the edges and twist at the top to seal it. Line a steamer with the cabbage leaves. Place the dumplings on the cabbage and steam, covered, for 20 minutes.

4 To make the sauce, pound the garlic, chillies and sugar using a mortar and pestle. Stir in the lime juice and pulp, nam pla, water and mix well. Serve the sauce with the dumplings.

500 g (1 lb) plain flour

300 ml (½ pint) water

1 small cabbage, separated into leaves

Filling:

500 g (1 lb) boneless, skinless chicken breasts

250 g (8 oz) can bamboo shoots, drained and chopped

3 spring onions, finely chopped

3 slices fresh root ginger, peeled and finely chopped

2 teaspoons sugar

2 teaspoons light soy sauce

2 tablesoons dry sherry

2 tablespoons Chicken Stock (see page 9)

1 teaspoon sesame oil

salt

Tangy Chilli Sauce:

2 garlic cloves

4 dried red chillies or 1 fresh red chilli

5 teaspoons sugar

juice and pulp of ¼ lime

4 tablespoons fish sauce (nam pla) or soy sauce

5 tablespoons water

Serves 8

Preparation time: 45 minutes

Cooking time: 20 minutes

375 g (12 oz) chicken off the bone, skin removed

2 tablespoons Chinese wine or dry sherry

4 spring onions, chopped

2.5 cm (1 inch) piece fresh root ginger, peeled and finely chopped

2 tablespoons sunflower oil

1–2 garlic cloves, sliced

2 celery sticks, sliced diagonally

1 small green pepper, cored, deseeded and sliced lengthways

2 tablespoons light soy sauce

juice of ½ lemon

rind of 2 lemons, shredded

¼ teaspoon chilli powder

To Garnish (optional):

lemon slices

parsley sprigs

Serves 4

Preparation time: 10 minutes, plus marinating

Cooking time: about 10 minutes

1 Cut the chicken into 7 cm (3 inch) strips. Mix the wine or sherry with the spring onions and ginger.

2 Add the chicken and toss well to coat the pieces. Set aside to marinate for 15 minutes.

3 Heat the oil in a wok or large frying pan and add the garlic, celery and green pepper. Stir-fry for 1 minute. Add the marinated chicken and cook for a further 5 minutes.

4 Stir in the soy sauce, lemon juice and rind and the chilli powder, and cook for 1 minute more.

5 Transfer to a warmed serving dish and garnish with lemon slices and a sprig of parsley, if liked.

stir-fried lemon chicken with vegetables

club sandwich

1 Cook the bacon under a preheated moderate grill for 5–7 minutes, turning once, until crisp on both sides. Remove and drain on paper towels.

2 Toast the bread on both sides. Place the toast on a large board or work surface and spread one side of each slice with 1 tablespoon of mayonnaise.

3 Arrange two lettuce leaves on each of two slices of toast and sprinkle with salt and pepper to taste. Arrange one slice of turkey on top of the lettuce, then another slice of toast, with the mayonnaise side up. Arrange the remaining lettuce leaves on top and add the tomato slices and bacon.

4 Cover with the remaining two slices of toast, mayonnaise side down. Pierce the sandwiches with long toothpicks. Serve immediately.

6 strips bacon

6 slices multi-grain bread

6 tablespoons mayonnaise

8 lettuce leaves

2 large slices cooked turkey

2 tomatoes, thinly sliced

salt and pepper

Makes 2

Preparation time: about 10 minutes

Cooking time: 5–7 minutes

375 g (12 oz) boneless, skinless smoked chicken, cut into chunks

1 pink grapefruit

2 small oranges

½ cucumber, thinly sliced

1 small fennel bulb, trimmed and thinly sliced (optional)

about 50 g (2 oz) frisé

about 50 g (2 oz) lamb's lettuce or watercress

pink peppercorns (optional)

salt and pepper

Yogurt Dressing:

150 ml (¼ pint) plain yogurt

1 tablespoon lemon juice

1 teaspoon clear honey

½ teaspoon Dijon mustard

salt and pepper

Serves 4

Preparation time: 20 minutes

---

1 To make the dressing, put all the ingredients into a small bowl and beat with a wooden spoon until smooth.

2 Put the chicken pieces into a large bowl. Using a small sharp knife, peel the grapefruit and oranges, taking care to remove all the pith. Working over a bowl to catch the juices, segment the flesh. Set the juice aside. Add the citrus fruit to the chicken with the cucumber and fennel. Toss lightly to combine.

3 Divide the salad leaves between four individual plates and arrange the chicken mixture on top. To serve, stir the reserved citrus juices and the pink peppercorns, if using, into the dressing, and pour over the salad.

smoked chicken & citrus salad

■ This yogurt dressing is low in fat and calories. It can be varied according to taste by adding chopped herbs or pickles, garlic, curry paste or finely grated orange rind.

28

chicken & avocado salad

1 Place the chicken in a mixing bowl with the onion, apple, walnuts and sultanas.

2 Add the sliced avocados to the chicken mixture.

3 Mix the dressing ingredients together, pour over the chicken and avocado mixture and stir well. Place the salad leaves on four plates and top with the chicken and avocado mixture. Serve the salad sprinkled with chopped dill.

■ Smoked or Tandoori chicken can be used instead of plain chicken in this salad, providing a variation in the flavour.

250 g (8 oz) boneless, skinless cooked chicken, shredded

1 small red onion, thinly sliced

1 small red apple, thinly sliced

25 g (1 oz) walnuts, roughly chopped

1 tablespoon sultanas

2 avocados, peeled, stoned and sliced

Dressing:

1 tablespoon French mustard

3 tablespoons olive oil

1 tablespoon white wine vinegar

1 teaspoon caster sugar

1 garlic clove, crushed

1 teaspoon chopped thyme

To Serve:

1 bag of mixed salad leaves

1 tablespoon chopped dill

Serves 4

Preparation time: 5 minutes

chicken pizza mexicana •

spicy chicken casserole •

chicken sautéed with mushrooms •

country chicken with peppers & tomatoes •

chicken & lemon croquettes •

cashew chicken •

hot chicken liver salad •

chargrilled chicken with tomato-chilli salsa •

chicken & tomato pasta •

chicken & orange shells •

chicken & pea pasta bake •

pasta with chicken, cream & mushroom sauce •

shredded chicken & celery •

grilled chicken with cheese •

warm salad of chicken & red pepper •

quick &
easy

325 g (11 oz) boneless, skinless chicken, cut into 1½ cm (¾ inch) pieces

finely grated rind of 2 limes

1 teaspoon coriander seeds, crushed

3 tablespoons olive oil

1 ready-made 30 cm (12 inch) pizza base

125 g (4 oz) mozzarella cheese, grated

75 g (3 oz) smoked cheese, grated

75 g (3 oz) canned red kidney beans

75 g (3 oz) frozen sweetcorn kernels, thawed

1 fresh chilli, deseeded and finely chopped

½ red onion, very thinly sliced

½ red pepper, cored, deseeded and very thinly sliced

salt and pepper

coarsely chopped fresh coriander, to garnish

1 Rub the chicken with the lime rind and coriander seeds. Heat 2 tablespoons of the oil in a frying pan, add the chicken pieces and stir-fry for 3 minutes.

2 Put the pizza base on a greased perforated pizza pan. Sprinkle with the mozzarella and smoked cheese, then add the drained and rinsed kidney beans, sweetcorn and chilli. Arrange the onion and pepper slices on top, along with the chicken. Drizzle with the remaining oil and season to taste with salt and pepper.

3 Bake in a preheated oven, 240°C (475°F), Gas Mark 9, for about 20 minutes. Serve immediately, with a tomato and onion salad, if liked and garnished with coriander.

Makes 1 x 30 cm (12 inch) pizza	
Preparation time: 15 minutes	
Cooking time: about 25 minutes	

chicken pizza mexicana

spicy chicken casserole

1 Spread the flour on a plate. Add the coriander, cinnamon, cloves and salt and pepper and mix thoroughly, then use to coat the chicken quarters.

2 Heat 2 tablespoons of the oil in a large flameproof casserole, add the chicken quarters and sauté over a moderate heat for 7–10 minutes until golden on all sides. Remove with a slotted spoon and set aside on a plate.

3 Heat the remaining oil in the casserole, add the celery, onion and garlic and fry over a moderate heat, stirring frequently, for about 5 minutes until the vegetables are softened but not brown. Add the tomatoes and tomato purée and stir well to mix, then pour in the stock. Increase the heat and bring to the boil, stirring to break up the tomatoes as much as possible. Return the chicken to the casserole with the juices that have collected on the plate. Cover and simmer over a gentle heat, stirring occasionally, for 40 minutes or until the chicken is tender when pierced in the thickest part with a fork.

4 Gently stir in the chopped fresh coriander, and adjust the seasoning if necessary. Serve the casserole hot with boiled rice or new potatoes.

2 tablespoons plain flour

1 teaspoon ground coriander

½ teaspoon ground cinnamon

¼ teaspoon ground cloves

4 chicken quarters, skinned

3 tablespoons virgin olive oil

2 celery sticks, finely chopped

1 onion, finely chopped

2 garlic cloves, crushed

400 g (13 oz) can chopped or crushed tomatoes

1 tablespoon tomato purée

300 ml (½ pint) hot Chicken Stock (see page 9)

2–3 tablespoons chopped fresh coriander

salt and pepper

Serves 4

Preparation time: 15 minutes

Cooking time: about 1 hour

1 Heat the oil in a large saucepan. Add the chicken thighs or drumsticks and brown all over. Season with salt and plenty of pepper. Lower the heat and continue to cook for about 10 minutes, stirring frequently, until the chicken is tender. Remove with a slotted spoon and set aside.

2 Increase the heat and add the butter. As soon as it has melted, add the garlic, onion and mushrooms and stir-fry over a high heat for about 5 minutes until the mushrooms are just cooked. Stir in the breadcrumbs, parsley and reserved chicken and cook for 2–3 minutes to heat the chicken through.

3 Toss the red and yellow peppers with the vinaigrette and arrange them on four warmed serving plates. Place the chicken on the peppers and serve at once, topped with the sautéed mushrooms.

2 tablespoons sunflower oil

8 chicken thighs or drumsticks

25 g (1 oz) butter

2 large garlic cloves, crushed

1 small onion, finely chopped

175 g (6 oz) mushrooms, sliced

2 tablespoons dried breadcrumbs

2 tablespoons chopped flat leaf parsley

2 red peppers, cored, deseeded and thinly sliced

2 yellow peppers, cored, deseeded and thinly sliced

3 tablespoons vinaigrette dressing

salt and pepper

Serves 4

Preparation time: 10 minutes

Cooking time: about 20 minutes

chicken sautéed with mushrooms

■ The term 'sauté' is derived from the French verb *sauter* which means 'to jump.' It describes the way in which the food is cooked at a high temperature and the pan is shaken to brown the food.

1 Coat the chicken pieces in the seasoned flour in a strong plastic bag. Shake off the excess flour. Heat the oil in a large frying pan, add the onions and sauté for 3 minutes. Add the chicken and cook until golden on all sides.

2 Add the peppers, garlic, tomatoes, red wine, oregano and bay leaf to the pan. Cover and simmer gently for 40 minutes. Spoon the chicken and vegetables on to a warmed serving dish and garnish with the black olives. Serve at once.

4 chicken quarters

seasoned flour, for dredging

4 tablespoons corn oil

2 onions, finely chopped

2 green peppers, cored, deseeded and sliced

2 garlic cloves, crushed

500 g (1 lb) plum tomatoes, chopped

600 ml (1 pint) red wine

1 tablespoon dried oregano

1 bay leaf

pitted black olives, to garnish

Serves 4	
Preparation time: 15 minutes	
Cooking time: about 50 minutes	

country chicken with peppers & tomatoes

chicken
& lemon
croquettes

1   Melt the butter in a saucepan, sprinkle in the flour and cook, stirring, for 1–2 minutes. Remove from the heat and beat in the milk, a little at a time, then return to the heat and bring to the boil, stirring, until the mixture is very thick and smooth.

2   Remove the pan from the heat and add the chicken, tarragon or parsley, half the lemon rind and salt and pepper to taste. Beat well to mix. Turn the mixture out on to a plate, spread it out evenly and leave until quite cold.

3   Form the mixture into 4 oval croquettes. Pour the beaten egg on to a shallow plate, and spread the breadcrumbs mixed with the remaining lemon rind on another. Coat the croquettes first in the beaten egg then in the breadcrumbs. Press the breadcrumbs on firmly so that they stick to the croquettes. Chill for at least 30 minutes.

4   Heat the oil in a large frying pan until hot but not smoking. Add the croquettes and fry for 3 minutes on each side until the breadcrumbs are golden brown and crisp. Remove with a fish slice and drain on kitchen paper. Serve with a few lemon wedges and tarragon or parsley sprigs.

25 g (1 oz) butter

2 tablespoons plain flour

150 ml (¼ pint) milk

250 g (8 oz) boneless, skinless cooked chicken, finely chopped

2–3 teaspoons finely chopped tarragon or parsley

finely grated rind of 2 lemons

1 egg, beaten

about 75 g (3 oz) fine dried breadcrumbs

2 tablespoons rapeseed oil

salt and pepper

To Serve:

lemon wedges

tarragon or parsley sprigs

Serves 4
Preparation time: 30 minutes, plus cooling and chilling
Cooking time: 10 minutes

1 egg white, lightly beaten

4 tablespoons Chinese rice wine or dry sherry

2 teaspoons cornflour

375 g (12 oz) boneless, skinless chicken, cut into 1 cm (½ inch) cubes

3 tablespoons sunflower oil

4 spring onions, chopped

2 garlic cloves, chopped

2.5 cm (1 inch) piece fresh root ginger, peeled and finely chopped

1 tablespoon light soy sauce

125 g (4 oz) unsalted cashew nuts

Serves 4

Preparation time: 10–15 minutes

Cooking time: about 8 minutes

1 Place the egg white, half of the wine or sherry and the cornflour in a bowl and stir until well blended and smooth. Add the chicken cubes and toss until evenly coated.

2 Heat the oil in a wok or large frying pan. Add the spring onions, garlic and ginger and stir-fry for 30 seconds. Add the chicken and cook for about 5 minutes. Pour in the remaining wine or sherry and the soy sauce and stir well. Add the cashew nuts to the wok and cook for a further 30 seconds. Serve at once.

cashew chicken

1 Heat the butter with the oil in a large frying pan. Add the chicken livers and cook over a high heat for 3–4 minutes, stirring frequently, until browned on the outside but still lightly pink inside. Remove from the heat and stir in the vinegar and mustard, with salt and pepper to taste.

2 Arrange the salad leaves on 4 individual serving plates.

3 Spoon the hot chicken liver mixture on top of the salad leaves and sprinkle with the spring onions and parsley sprigs. Serve immediately.

25 g (1 oz) butter

5 tablespoons light olive oil

500 g (1 lb) chicken livers, halved

2 tablespoons red wine vinegar

1 teaspoon wholegrain mustard

about 250 g (8 oz) mixed salad leaves (e.g. red oakleaf, frisé, radicchio, chicory)

2 spring onions, thinly sliced

flat leaf parsley sprigs

salt and pepper

Serves 4

Preparation time: 20 minutes

Cooking time: about 5 minutes

hot chicken liver salad

40

chargrilled chicken with tomato-chilli salsa

1 Put the chicken breasts on a board, cover with greaseproof paper and pound with a rolling pin to flatten slightly. Remove the paper and place the chicken in a shallow dish. Whisk together the olive oil, lime rind and juice and pepper to taste. Brush over the chicken, then cover and marinate at room temperature for about 1 hour.

2 To make the salsa, put all the ingredients in a bowl with salt and pepper to taste and mix well. Cover and chill until ready to serve.

3 Brush a little of the oil from the chicken on a griddle pan and place over a moderate heat until hot. Put the chicken breasts and the remaining oil on the pan and cook for 3–5 minutes on each side or until the chicken feels tender when pierced with a skewer or fork.

4 Serve the chicken on a bed of salad leaves, garnished with lime wedges and coriander sprigs. Serve the salsa on top.

■ Chillies vary enormously in their 'hotness' but generally, the smaller they are, the hotter they will be.

2 large boneless, skinless, chicken breasts

4 tablespoons extra virgin olive oil

finely grated rind and juice of 2 limes

salt and pepper

mixed salad leaves, to serve

Tomato-Chilli Salsa:

250 g (8 oz) cherry tomatoes, quartered lengthways

1–2 fresh red or green chillies, deseeded and very finely diced

2 garlic cloves, crushed

3 tablespoons extra virgin olive oil

juice of 1 lime

2 tablespoons chopped coriander

½ teaspoon sugar

To Garnish:

lime wedges

coriander sprigs

Serves 2

Preparation time: 15 minutes, plus marinating

Cooking time: about 10 minutes

375 g (12 oz) dried penne, conchiglie or gnocchi

Sauce:

2 tablespoons olive oil

250 g (8 oz) boneless, skinless chicken breasts, diced

1 large onion, finely chopped

3 celery sticks, diced

2 carrots, diced

2 teaspoons dried oregano

125 ml (4 fl oz) red wine

400 g (13 oz) can chopped tomatoes

salt and pepper

To Garnish:

1 tablespoon oregano leaves

Parmesan shavings

Serves 4–6
Preparation time: 10 minutes
Cooking time: 20 minutes

1 To make the sauce, heat the oil in a frying pan and fry the chicken pieces, stirring occasionally, until lightly coloured. Add the onion, celery and carrots and cook for 5 minutes until softened.

2 Add the oregano, wine and tomatoes and season to taste with salt and pepper. Bring the sauce to the boil, cover the pan and simmer for 10 minutes.

3 Meanwhile, cook the pasta in lightly salted boiling water according to packet instructions or until just tender. Drain and toss with half of the sauce. Transfer the pasta to a warmed serving dish, spoon over the remaining sauce and serve immediately, garnished with oregano leaves and Parmesan shavings.

chicken & tomato pasta

chicken & orange shells

1 Put the chicken, orange rind and juice, the egg yolk, cream and cayenne into a food processor with salt and pepper to taste and process for 1 minute or until smooth. Whisk the egg white in a grease-free bowl until firm peaks form, then fold it into the chicken mixture.

2 Spoon a little of the filling into each pasta shell. Arrange the shells over the base of a steamer and steam for 15 minutes or until the chicken filling has set.

3 Divide the salad leaves between four serving plates and place the shells on top. Drizzle with the olive oil and garnish with the fennel sprigs and basil leaves.

250 g (8 oz) cooked boneless, skinless, chicken breasts, roughly chopped

grated rind of 1 orange

2 tablespoons orange juice

1 egg, separated

3 tablespoons double cream

½ teaspoon cayenne pepper

16 large dried pasta shells, cooked

1 bag of mixed salad leaves

4 tablespoons olive oil

salt and pepper

To Garnish:

fennel sprigs

basil leaves

Serves 4
Preparation time: 10 minutes
Cooking time: 15 minutes

1½ tablespoons olive oil

300 g (10 oz) dried pasta shells or other pasta shapes

250 g (8 oz) cooked chicken breast, sliced into strips

125 g (4 oz) fresh peas, shelled

1 garlic clove, crushed

2 tablespoons torn basil leaves

1 tablespoon chopped thyme

3 tablespoons chopped parsley

½ small red pepper, cored, deseeded and chopped

50 g (2 oz) freshly grated Parmesan cheese

salt and pepper

basil sprigs, to garnish

1 Bring a large pan of water to the boil. Add ½ tablespoon of the oil and a generous pinch of salt. Cook the pasta shells for 8–12 minutes until just tender.

2 Heat the remaining oil in a large frying pan, add the chicken and sauté gently for 2 minutes. Stir in the peas, garlic, basil, thyme, parsley and red pepper, and cook, stirring, for a further 2 minutes.

3 Pour the chicken mixture into a large greased ovenproof dish, add the pasta shells, season with salt and pepper and toss well. Sprinkle with the grated Parmesan and bake in a preheated oven, 200°C (400°F), Gas Mark 6, for 20 minutes. Garnish with basil sprigs and serve immediately.

Serves 4

Preparation time: 10 minutes

Cooking time: about 35 minutes

chicken & pea pasta bake

pasta with chicken, cream & mushroom sauce

1 Put the chicken in a saucepan with the onion, carrot, bouquet garni and peppercorns. Pour in the water and add the sherry, if using. Bring to the boil, then lower the heat, cover and poach the chicken for about 20 minutes until just tender when pierced with a fork.

2 Meanwhile, melt the butter in a separate pan, add the mushrooms, garlic, rosemary and salt and pepper to taste, and sauté over a moderate heat, stirring constantly, for 5 minutes or until the juices run clear. Remove from the heat and using a slotted spoon, transfer the mushrooms to a bowl.

3 Bring a large pan of water to the boil. Add the oil and a generous pinch of salt. Cook the pasta for 8–12 minutes, or according to packet instructions, until just tender.

3 part-boned chicken breasts

1 small onion, quartered

1 carrot, roughly chopped

1 bouquet garni

a few black peppercorns

300 ml (½ pint) water

2 tablespoons dry sherry (optional)

50 g (2 oz) butter

250 g (8 oz) button mushrooms, thinly sliced

2 garlic cloves, crushed

1 teaspoon chopped rosemary

1 teaspoon virgin olive oil

375 g (12 oz) dried pasta shapes (e.g. bows, penne, spirals)

1½ tablespoons plain flour

150 ml (¼ pint) double cream

salt and pepper

rosemary sprigs, to garnish

Serves 4
Preparation time: 30 minutes
Cooking time: about 30 minutes

4 Meanwhile, lift the chicken out of the poaching liquid, then strain the liquid into a jug. Cut the chicken into strips, discarding the skin and bones.

5 Return the mushroom cooking liquid to the heat, sprinkle in the flour and cook for 1–2 minutes, stirring. Add the chicken poaching liquid a little at a time, beating well after each addition.

6 Bring to the boil, stirring. Lower the heat and stir in the cream. Add the chicken, mushrooms and salt and pepper. Mix well, then simmer, stirring, for 5 minutes or until thickened.

7 Drain the pasta and turn into a warmed serving bowl. Pour in the sauce and toss to mix with the pasta. Serve hot, garnished with rosemary.

■ Use white button mushrooms for this sauce as dark ones will spoil its delicate appearance.

shredded chicken & celery

1 Place the chicken in a bowl. Add the salt, egg white and cornflour and mix thoroughly.

2 Heat the oil in a wok or large frying pan and add the chicken. Stir-fry over a moderate heat until the chicken is lightly and evenly browned. Remove the chicken with a slotted spoon and set aside on a plate.

3 Increase the heat and, when the oil is very hot, add the ginger and spring onions followed by the celery and green pepper. Stir-fry for about 30 seconds over a high heat.

4 Return the chicken shreds to the wok with the soy sauce and sherry. Mix well and cook for a further 1–1½ minutes, stirring all the time. Transfer to a warmed serving dish and serve immediately.

250 g (8 oz) boneless, skinless chicken breasts, cut into shreds

½ teaspoon salt

1 egg white

1 tablespoon cornflour

4 tablespoons vegetable oil

4 slices of fresh root ginger, peeled and cut into thin strips

2 spring onions, cut into thin strips

1 small celery stick, cut into strips

1 green pepper, cored, deseeded and cut into thin strips

2 tablespoons soy sauce

1 tablespoon dry sherry

Serves 3–4

Preparation time: 15 minutes

Cooking time: 7–8 minutes

1   Cut four pieces of foil 30 cm (12 inches) square. Cut three slits in each chicken breast and arrange them on the foil.

2   Mix together the vegetable oil, lemon juice, thyme and salt and pepper. Draw the foil around the chicken, pour over the sauce and seal the parcels.

3   Cook the chicken parcels under a preheated moderate grill, turning them once, for 30 minutes until the juices run clear when pierced with a skewer.

4   Open the parcels, arrange the ham, cheese, then tomatoes on the chicken breasts and spoon over a little sauce. Grill the topping under a high heat for 3–4 minutes until the cheese melts. Serve immediately.

4 boneless, skinless chicken breasts

4 tablespoons vegetable oil

1 tablespoon lemon juice

1 tablespoon dried thyme

125 g (4 oz) cooked ham, thinly sliced

50 g (2 oz) Gruyère cheese, thinly sliced

2 large tomatoes, sliced

salt and pepper

Serves 4

Preparation time: 5 minutes

Cooking time: 35 minutes

grilled chicken with cheese

warm salad of chicken & red pepper

1 Heat the oil in a large frying pan, add the chicken strips and red pepper and fry, stirring frequently, for 10 minutes or until tender.

2 Whisk the dressing ingredients until thickened. Tear the lettuce leaves and put in a large salad bowl.

3 When the chicken and pepper strips are tender, remove them with a slotted spoon and place on top of the lettuce.

4 Pour the dressing into the pan, increase the heat to high and stir until sizzling. Pour the hot dressing over the salad and toss to combine. Serve immediately, accompanied by good, crusty French bread.

2 tablespoons extra virgin olive oil

500 g (1 lb) chicken breast fillets, cut diagonally into thin strips

1 red pepper, cored, deseeded and cut lengthways into thin strips

2 Little Gem lettuces, leaves separated

Dressing:

3 tablespoons extra virgin olive oil

2 tablespoons lemon juice

1 garlic clove, crushed

1 teaspoon Dijon mustard

salt and pepper

Serves 4
Preparation time: 10 minutes
Cooking time: 10 minutes

spicy chicken braised with coconut juice ●

hot & sour chicken soup ●

tex-mex chicken with salsa ●

irish chicken frigasse ●

balti chicken ●

jamaican jerked chicken ●

chicken couscous ●

pollo alla cacciatora ●

burmese chicken curry & cellophane noodles ●

moroccan tagine ●

caribbean curry ●

italian roast chicken ●

spanish paella ●

good luck chicken ●

jambalaya ●

ginger chicken with honey ●

coast to coast

2 tablespoons oil

1 kg (2 lb) chicken, cut into serving pieces

1 tablespoon Chinese wine or dry sherry

2 tablespoons soy sauce

salt and pepper

2 onions, cut into quarters

3 spring onions, chopped

3 garlic cloves, chopped

2 tablespoons curry paste

2 teaspoons curry powder

300 ml (½ pint) water

3 potatoes, cut into 2.5 cm (1 inch) pieces

2 carrots, cut into 2.5 cm (1 inch) pieces

4 tablespoons coconut juice

2 tablespoons plain flour

2 teaspoons sugar

a few strips of green pepper, to garnish

1 Heat 1 tablespoon of the oil in a wok or large frying pan. Add the chicken and stir-fry until browned. Add the wine or sherry, soy sauce, salt and pepper. Stir-fry for a few seconds, then add the onions. Stir-fry for 30 seconds, then transfer to a saucepan.

2 Heat the remaining oil in the pan. Add the spring onions and garlic, then add the curry paste and powder. Stir-fry for 30 seconds, then add the water. Pour over the chicken and add the potatoes and carrots. Bring to the boil, cover and simmer for 20 minutes, or until the chicken is tender. Mix the coconut juice with the flour and sugar and stir into the pan. Cook until the sauce is thickened. Serve, garnished with strips of pepper.

Serves 4

Preparation time: 15 minutes

Cooking time: 30–40 minutes

spicy chicken braised with coconut juice

1 Cover the dried shiitake mushrooms in warm water and leave to soak for about 20 minutes. Drain and reserve the soaking liquid. Thinly slice the reconstituted mushrooms.

2 Bring the stock to the boil in a large saucepan over a moderate heat. Add the reserved mushroom liquid, the soy sauce, rice wine or sherry, sugar, chilli and ginger. Lower the heat, add the mushrooms and simmer for 20 minutes.

3 Add the shredded chicken, spring onions and carrots and simmer for a further 5 minutes. Add salt and pepper to taste and serve hot, garnished with coriander leaves if liked.

15 g (½ oz) dried shiitake mushrooms

2 litres (3½ pints) Chicken Stock (see page 9)

2 tablespoons soy sauce

2 tablespoons Chinese rice wine or dry sherry

1 teaspoon soft brown sugar

1 fresh green chilli, deseeded and very finely chopped

5 cm (2 inch) piece of fresh root ginger, peeled and very finely shredded

about 250 g (8 oz) cooked boneless, skinless chicken, finely shredded

6 spring onions, finely shredded

2 carrots, grated

salt and pepper

coriander leaves, to garnish (optional)

Serves 4–6

Preparation time: 10 minutes, plus soaking

Cooking time: about 30 minutes

hot & sour chicken soup

tex-mex chicken with salsa

1 Score the chicken breasts diagonally in several places with a sharp knife. Whisk together the olive oil, lime rind and juice and the cumin. Brush over the chicken, working it into the incisions in the flesh. Cover and marinate for about 1 hour.

2 To make the salsa, put all the ingredients into a bowl and stir well to mix. Cover and chill until ready to serve.

3 Remove the chicken from the marinade, reserving the marinade. Put the chicken under a preheated hot grill or over a barbecue and cook for 5–7 minutes on each side or until the chicken feels tender when pierced with a fork, brushing frequently with the marinade.

4 To serve, slice the chicken diagonally, along the lines of the first incisions. Arrange alongside the salsa on warmed plates. Serve immediately. Corn tortillas and avocado are the traditional accompaniments.

6 large boneless, skinless chicken breasts

6 tablespoons extra virgin olive oil

finely grated rind and juice of 2 limes

¾ teaspoon ground cumin

Salsa:

500 g (1 lb) ripe tomatoes, skinned, deseeded and finely chopped

1 small onion, finely chopped

2 garlic cloves, crushed

1 hot green chilli, deseeded and finely chopped

3 tablespoons extra virgin olive oil

2 teaspoons wine vinegar

juice of 1 lime

¼ teaspoon salt

Serves 6
Preparation time: 15 minutes, plus marinating
Cooking time: 10–15 minutes

irish chicken frigasse

1 To make the sauce, melt the butter in a saucepan, stir in the flour and gradually add the stock and milk until blended. Bring to the boil, stirring constantly until thick and smooth and then cook for a few minutes.

2 Mix the egg yolk and cream and whisk into the sauce with the remaining ingredients. Fold in the chicken strips, stir in the mushrooms and onions and heat thoroughly.

3 Serve the chicken frigasse on a large flat dish garnished with the bacon rolls, lemon wedges, watercress and a dusting of paprika.

750 g (1½ lb) cooked boneless, skinless chicken breast, cut into thick strips

175 g (6 oz) button mushrooms, fried

16 pickling onions, peeled and blanched

Sauce:

50 g (2 oz) butter

50 g (2 oz) plain flour

300 ml (½ pint) Chicken Stock (see page 9)

300 ml (½ pint) milk

1 egg yolk

65 ml (2½ fl oz) double cream

1–2 tablespoons Worcestershire sauce

1 tablespoon mustard

1 teaspoon anchovy sauce

2 teaspoons capers

2 tablespoons finely chopped parsley

salt and pepper

To Garnish:

8 rashers of bacon, cut in half, rolled and grilled

4 lemon wedges

paprika

Serves 4–6

Preparation time: 20 minutes

Cooking time: 10–15 minutes

---

balti chicken

1 Dry-fry the peppercorns and fennel seeds in a wok or large frying pan over a gentle heat, stirring constantly, for 2–3 minutes until fragrant. Remove, then pound to a fine powder using a pestle and mortar. Heat the oil in the same pan, add the onion, ginger and garlic and fry gently, stirring frequently, for about 5 minutes until soft but not brown.

2 Add the powdered spices, garam masala, coriander, cumin, chilli and turmeric. Stir-fry this for 2–3 minutes, then add the water, coconut milk powder, lemon juice and ½ teaspoon salt. Bring to the boil, stirring, then add the cardamoms, cinnamon and bay leaf. Simmer, stirring occasionally, for about 15–20 minutes, until a glaze forms on the liquid.

3 Add the chicken, tomatoes and sugar and stir well. Cover and cook over a gentle heat for about 40 minutes, stirring occasionally, or until the chicken feels tender when pierced with a fork.

4 Discard the bay leaf and cinnamon stick, then taste, and add more salt if necessary. Serve hot, sprinkled with coriander leaves, and accompanied by some Indian bread.

½ teaspoon black peppercorns

½ teaspoon fennel seeds

2 tablespoons oil

1 onion, thinly sliced

2.5 cm (1 inch) piece of fresh root ginger, peeled and crushed

1 garlic clove, crushed

1 tablespoon garam masala

1 teaspoon ground coriander

1 teaspoon ground cumin

1 teaspoon chilli powder, or to taste

1 teaspoon turmeric

475 ml (16 fl oz) water

50 g (2 oz) coconut milk powder

1 tablespoon lemon juice

6 cardamon pods, bruised

5 cm (2 inch) cinnamon stick

1 bay leaf

1 kg (2 lb) boneless, skinless chicken thighs, cut into bite-sized pieces

4 ripe tomatoes, skinned, deseeded and roughly chopped

¼ teaspoon sugar

salt

coriander leaves, to garnish

Serves 4–6

Preparation time: 30 minutes

Cooking time: about 1 hour

1 First make the jerked seasoning. Pound the allspice berries, cinnamon and nutmeg using a pestle and mortar. Add the chilli, spring onions, bay leaf and salt and pepper to the mortar and pound to a thick paste. Stir the rum into the paste and mix well. Slash the chicken deeply on the skin side 2–3 times, and then rub the paste all over the chicken. Cover and marinate for 1–2 hours.

2 Meanwhile, make the pineapple chutney. Put all the ingredients into a saucepan and stir well. Place over a moderate heat and stir until the sugar has completely dissolved. Bring to the boil and then reduce the heat a little. Cook vigorously, stirring occasionally, until the chutney thickens.

3 Pour the chutney into sterilised glass jars and seal. If liked, it can be made in advance and kept for 2–3 weeks in a refrigerator.

4 Put the jerked chicken into a roasting tin and roast in a preheated oven, 200°C (400°F°), Gas Mark 6, for 20–30 minutes, or cook under a preheated hot grill. Serve with the pineapple chutney and some plain boiled rice.

6 chicken joints

Jerked Seasoning:

25 g (1 oz) allspice berries

5 cm (2 inch) cinnamon stick

1 teaspoon freshly grated nutmeg

1 fresh red chilli, deseeded and finely chopped

4 spring onions, thinly sliced

1 bay leaf, crumbled

1 tablespoon dark rum

salt and pepper

Pineapple Chutney:

2 fresh pineapples, peeled and chopped

2.5 cm (1 inch) piece of fresh root ginger, peeled and finely chopped

1 onion, finely chopped

1 fresh red chilli, deseeded and finely chopped

125 ml (4 fl oz) vinegar

250 g (8 oz) soft dark brown sugar

Serves 6

Preparation time: 20 minutes, plus marinating

Cooking time: 30–40 minutes

jamaican jerked chicken

62

chicken couscous

1 Heat the oil in a saucepan and quickly fry the onions, garlic and spices. Stir in the tomato purée, chickpeas and season to taste. Cover with water and bring to the boil. Simmer, stirring often, for 1 hour. Top up with water to cover the chickpeas.

2 Add the chicken pieces, cover and simmer for 20 minutes, stirring occasionally. Stir the carrots, parsnips and potatoes into the chicken and chickpeas, cover with water and bring to the boil. Put the couscous into a bowl and cover with boiling water. Add the cinnamon and orange flower water and stir.

3 Put the couscous and half the butter in a steamer on top of the saucepan. Cover and cook for 30 minutes, adding the courgettes and sultanas halfway through. Remove the couscous from the steamer and fork through the remaining butter. Serve the chicken and vegetables on the couscous and garnish with coriander.

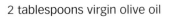

2 tablespoons virgin olive oil

2 onions, finely chopped

3 garlic cloves, finely chopped

2 teaspoons ground coriander

2 teaspoons cumin

2 teaspoons ground turmeric

2 teaspoons chilli powder

2 tablespoons tomato purée

125 g (4 oz) canned chickpeas

12 boneless, skinless chicken thighs, cut into large bite-sized pieces

4 carrots, thickly sliced

2 parsnips, thickly sliced

2 potatoes, cut into chunks

500 g (1 lb) couscous

½ teaspoon ground cinnamon

a few drops of orange flower water

50 g (2 oz) butter

4 courgettes, thickly sliced

2 tablespoons sultanas

salt and pepper

fresh coriander, to garnish

Serves 6–8

Preparation time: 40 minutes, plus soaking

Cooking time: about 2 hours

pollo alla cacciatora

1 Soak the dried mushrooms in the warm water for 20 minutes.

2 Meanwhile, heat the oil in a large flameproof casserole, add the chicken and sauté over a moderate heat for 7–10 minutes until golden on all sides. Remove with a slotted spoon and set aside on a plate.

3 Add the onion, carrot, celery and garlic to the casserole and gently fry, stirring frequently, for about 7–10 minutes until softened. Drain the mushrooms and reserve the soaking liquid. Finely chop the mushrooms and add them to the casserole with the reserved liquid and the wine. Increase the heat to moderate and stir until bubbling. Add the tomatoes with their juice, tomato purée, herbs, sugar and salt and pepper.

4 Return the chicken and juices to the casserole. Cover and simmer over a gentle heat, stirring occasionally, for 40 minutes or until the chicken is tender when pierced with a fork. Adjust the seasoning to taste. Serve hot, sprinkled with chopped parsley.

■ Italian dried mushrooms – Porcini – are available at most delicatessens and good supermarkets. Though expensive, they are full of flavour, so you need only a very small quantity.

15 g (½ oz) dried mushrooms

150 ml (¼ pint) warm water

2 tablespoons extra virgin olive oil

4 skinless chicken portions

1 onion, finely chopped

1 large carrot, finely chopped

1 large celery stick, finely chopped

2 garlic cloves, crushed

150 ml (¼ pint) Italian white wine

400 g (13 oz) can peeled plum tomatoes, roughly chopped

1 tablespoon tomato purée

1 teaspoon dried oregano

1 teaspoon dried mixed herbs

large pinch of sugar

salt and pepper

chopped flat leaf parsley, to garnish

Serves 4

Preparation time: 20 minutes

Cooking time: about 1 hour

burmese chicken curry & cellophane noodles

1 To make the spice paste, put all the ingredients in a food processor or blender and blend to a thick paste.

2 Heat the oil in a large heavy-based saucepan, add the spice paste and fry over a gentle heat, stirring constantly, for 5 minutes until softened. Add the chicken pieces and fry, stirring constantly, for a further 5 minutes to seal. Stir in the chilli powder, turmeric, salt, coconut milk and stock. Bring to the boil, then reduce the heat and simmer very gently, stirring occasionally, for 30 minutes or until the chicken is tender.

3 Stir the creamed coconut into the curry and then simmer over a moderate heat for 2–3 minutes, stirring constantly, until the creamed coconut has dissolved and thickened the sauce slightly. Taste and adjust the seasoning if necessary.

4 Drop the noodles into a pan of salted boiling water. Bring the water back to the boil and cook the noodles for 3 minutes. Drain the noodles and toss them with a little sesame oil.

5 To serve, divide the noodles between 4 deep soup bowls and ladle some chicken curry over each portion. Serve the accompaniments separately.

4 tablespoons groundnut oil

625 g (1¼ lb) boneless, skinless chicken breasts, cut into bite-sized pieces

1½ teaspoons chilli powder

½ teaspoon ground turmeric

½ teaspoon salt

600 ml (1 pint) coconut milk

300 ml (½ pint) Chicken Stock (see page 9)

50 g (2 oz) creamed coconut, chopped

375 g (12 oz) cellophane noodles

sesame oil

salt and pepper

Spice Paste:

4 large garlic cloves, chopped

2 onions, chopped

1 red chilli, deseeded and chopped

2.5 cm (1 inch) piece of fresh root ginger, peeled and chopped

1 teaspoon shrimp paste (optional)

Accompaniments:

3 spring onions, sliced

2 tablespoons fried onion flakes

2 tablespoons fresh coriander leaves

1 lemon, cut into wedges

Serves 4

Preparation time: 15 minutes

Cooking time: 50 minutes

1 Mix the turmeric, paprika and cinnamon in a small bowl and season with salt and pepper, then use to coat the chicken.

2 Heat the oil in a flameproof casserole, and cook the chicken over a moderate heat, stirring constantly, for 5 minutes until it changes colour. Remove the chicken pieces with a slotted spoon and set aside on a plate.

3 Add the onion, ginger and garlic to the casserole and cook over a gentle heat, stirring frequently, for about 5 minutes until softened. Gradually stir in the chicken stock, increase the heat to high and bring to the boil. Add the dried fruit and return the chicken and its juices to the casserole. Stir well to mix. Cover and simmer gently, stirring occasionally, for 40 minutes until the chicken is tender when pierced with a skewer or fork. Adjust the seasoning to taste. Serve hot, with plain boiled rice.

2 teaspoons ground turmeric

2 teaspoons paprika

1 teaspoon ground cinnamon

12 boneless, skinless chicken thighs, cut into bite-sized pieces

2 tablespoons extra virgin olive oil

1 onion, finely chopped

2.5 cm (1 inch) piece of fresh root ginger, peeled and crushed

1 garlic clove, crushed

600 ml (1 pint) Chicken Stock (see page 9)

250 g (8 oz) mixed dried fruit (prunes, apricots, apples, pears, peaches)

salt and pepper

Serves 4

Preparation time: 15 minutes

Cooking time: about 50 minutes

moroccan tagine

caribbean curry

1 Heat the oil in a heavy frying pan, add the chicken pieces and fry over a moderate heat until golden brown all over. Transfer to a flameproof casserole.

2 Add the onions, garlic and chilli to the frying pan and cook, stirring occasionally, over a moderate heat for about 5 minutes until the onions are soft. Add the curry powder, stir well and cook for 3 minutes, stirring. Add the aubergine, chayote, papaya and tomatoes, and cook for a further 2–3 minutes.

3 Put the curried mixture into the casserole and add the chicken stock and coconut milk. Cover and simmer for about 30 minutes, until the chicken is cooked and the vegetables are tender. Stir in the lime juice and rum or Madeira and season with salt and pepper. Serve with plain boiled rice and fried bananas.

5 tablespoons groundnut oil

2 kg (4 lb) chicken, cut into 6–8 serving pieces

2 onions, finely chopped

1 garlic clove, crushed

1 fresh red chilli, deseeded and finely chopped

2 tablespoons curry powder

250 g (8 oz) aubergine, peeled and cubed

1 chayote (see below), peeled and cubed

1 unripe papaya, peeled and sliced

2 tomatoes, skinned and chopped

150 ml (¼ pint) Chicken Stock (see page 9)

150 ml (¼ pint) coconut milk

2 tablespoons lime juice

1 tablespoon rum or Madeira

salt and pepper

Serves 4–6	
Preparation time: 10 minutes	
Cooking time: 50 minutes	

■ Chayotes are pale green, pear-shaped vegetables from the Caribbean. They can be found in large supermarkets or ethnic stores and have a similar flavour to marrow, which can be substituted if chayotes are unavailable.

coast to coast

1 Melt the butter in a heavy-based saucepan, chop the chicken giblets and add them to the pan. Fry gently for 10 minutes.

2 Add the breadcrumbs and fry until browned, then add the chopped tomatoes and simmer for 10 minutes. Remove from the heat and leave to cool.

3 Add the egg to the mixture with the cheese, milk, cream and salt and pepper to taste and mix thoroughly. Stuff the chicken with the mixture, putting the hard-boiled egg in the centre. Sew the opening securely with kitchen string.

4 Place the chicken in an oiled roasting tin, pour over the olive oil, sprinkle with salt and pepper and roast in a preheated oven, 200°C (400°F), Gas Mark 6, for 1½ hours or until the chicken is tender. Serve immediately.

25 g (1 oz) butter

1.5 kg (3 lb) oven-ready chicken with giblets

150 g (5 oz) dried breadcrumbs

3 tomatoes, skinned and chopped

1 egg, beaten

125 g (4 oz) pecorino cheese, grated

100 ml (3½ fl oz) milk

4 tablespoons single cream

1 hard-boiled egg

4 tablespoons olive oil

salt and pepper

Serves 6

Preparation time: 30 minutes

Cooking time: 1½–2 hours

italian roast chicken

spanish paella

1 Scrub the mussels with a small stiff brush and scrape off the beards and the barnacles with a small sharp knife. Discard any open mussels.

2 Slice 2 garlic cloves and crush the remainder. Put the slices into a saucepan with the herbs, wine, 150 ml (¼ pint) of the stock and salt and pepper. Add the mussels, cover and bring to the boil. Shake the pan and simmer for 5 minutes until they open. Remove the mussels and set aside, discarding any which remain closed. Strain the liquid and reserve.

3 Heat half of the oil and sauté the squid for 5 minutes, stirring. Add the onion, red pepper and crushed garlic and cook, stirring, for 5 minutes. Add the mussel cooking liquid, tomatoes and salt and pepper. Bring to the boil stirring, then simmer, stirring, for 15–20 minutes. Transfer to a bowl.

4 Heat the remaining oil in the pan and sauté the chicken for 5 minutes. Add the rice and stir briefly. Stir in the squid mixture. Add one third of the remaining stock and bring to the boil, stirring. Boil for 3–4 minutes, cover, and simmer for 30 minutes. Add more stock as needed and stir, to cook evenly. Cook until the chicken and rice are tender and the liquid is absorbed.

5 Add the peas and prawns and simmer, stirring, for 5 minutes, adding stock if needed. Add the mussels, cover with foil and cook for 5 minutes. Serve immediately.

1 kg (2 lb) fresh mussels

4 garlic cloves

1 bunch of fresh mixed herbs

150 ml (¼ pint) dry white wine

about 2 litres (3½ pints) Chicken Stock (see page 9)

4 tablespoons extra virgin olive oil

4 small squid, cleaned and sliced into rings

1 large onion, finely chopped

1 red pepper, cored, deseeded and chopped

4 large ripe tomatoes, skinned, deseeded and chopped

12 skinless, boneless chicken thighs, cut into bite-sized pieces

500 g (1 lb) short-grain rice

125 g (4 oz) fresh or frozen peas

12 large raw prawns, peeled, with tails left intact

salt and pepper

Serves 6

Preparation time: about 40 minutes

Cooking time: about 1¼ hours

good luck chicken

1 Heat the oil and fry the chicken breasts for 10–15 minutes, turning occasionally. When cooked, drain and sprinkle with the five spice powder. Cut into shreds and stir in the bean sprouts. Cut the spring onions into shreds and add to the chicken mixture. Season with salt and pepper.

2 Cut the filo pastry into twenty 10 x 18 cm (4 x 7 inch) rectangles. Spoon a little chicken mixture along the shorter edge of each one and sprinkle with soy sauce. Tuck the sides over the filling and roll the pastry to enclose the filling. Mix the flour with a little water to make the paste, brush along the edge of the roll and press to seal.

3 Heat the oil in a wok or large frying pan and cook the rolls in batches for about 4–6 minutes. Drain on kitchen paper and serve at once.

2 teaspoons sesame oil

3 boneless, skinless chicken breasts

2 teaspoons five spice powder

125 g (4 oz) bean sprouts

2 spring onions

3 sheets of filo pastry

soy sauce

2 teaspoons plain flour

water, to mix

sunflower oil, for deep-frying

salt and pepper

Makes about 20

Preparation time: 20 minutes

Cooking time: 20–25 minutes

jambalaya

1 Discard any open mussels. Put the wine, water, bouquet garni, garlic, mussels and salt and pepper into a large saucepan. Cover and bring to the boil. Shake the pan and simmer for 5 minutes or until the mussels open. Remove from the liquid and set aside, discarding any which remain closed. Strain the liquid and reserve.

2 Heat the oil in a casserole and fry the chicken and chorizo for 5 minutes. Remove and set aside. Add the onions, celery and peppers and fry for 5 minutes. Add the tomatoes, herbs and cayenne and stir. Add the mussel liquid and the stock or water. Bring to the boil, stirring. Add the rice, bay leaves, salt and pepper, and stir.

3 Return the chicken, chorizo and juices to the casserole, cover and simmer for 40 minutes, adding stock as needed. Discard the bay leaves. Add the mussels to the chicken and rice, cover and heat for 5 minutes, then serve.

500 g (1 lb) fresh mussels, scrubbed and debearded

150 ml (¼ pint) dry white wine

150 ml (¼ pint) water

1 bouquet garni

2 garlic cloves, crushed

2 tablespoons rapeseed oil

1.5 kg (3 lb) oven-ready chicken, giblets removed, cut into 8 pieces

175 g (6 oz) chorizo sausage, chopped

2 onions, finely chopped

2 celery sticks, finely chopped

1 green pepper, cored, deseeded and chopped

1 red pepper, cored, deseeded and chopped

400 g (13 oz) can chopped tomatoes

1 teaspoon dried thyme

1 teaspoon dried oregano

1 teaspoon cayenne pepper

about 600 ml (1 pint) hot Chicken Stock (see page 9) or water

500 g (1 lb) long-grain rice

2 bay leaves, broken up

salt and pepper

Serves 6

Preparation time: 40 minutes

Cooking time: about 1 hour

ginger chicken with honey

1 Put the spring onions into a bowl, cover with cold water and leave to soak until required. Mix the chopped ginger with a little cold water, then drain and squeeze to remove its hotness. Rinse under cold running water and drain well.

2 Heat the oil in a wok or large frying pan over a moderate heat. Add the chicken with the livers. Stir-fry for 5 minutes, then remove with a slotted spoon and set aside.

3 Drain the mushrooms and squeeze them dry. Discard the stalks. Add the onion to the wok and fry gently until soft. Add the garlic and mushrooms and stir-fry for 1 minute. Return the cooked chicken and chicken livers to the wok.

4 Mix the soy sauce and honey until blended. Pour over the chicken and stir well. Add the drained ginger and stir-fry for 2–3 minutes. Add the drained spring onions, and transfer to a serving dish. This dish tastes even better if it is cooked the day before and then reheated.

■ Dried Chinese black mushrooms are available from oriental shops and large supermarkets. Other dried mushrooms or shiitake mushrooms can be substituted.

5 spring onions, sliced into 1 cm (½ inch) pieces

50 g (2 oz) piece of fresh root ginger, peeled and finely chopped

2 tablespoons vegetable oil

3 boneless, skinless chicken breasts, thinly sliced

3 chicken livers, chopped

2 tablespoons dried Chinese black mushrooms, soaked in warm water for 20 minutes

1 onion, sliced

3 garlic cloves, crushed

2 tablespoons soy sauce

1 tablespoon clear honey

Serves 4

Preparation time: 15 minutes

Cooking time: 15 minutes

chicken galantine •

chicken suprêmes with roast peppers •

chicken with 40 garlic cloves •

chicken & red pesto roulades •

chicken with white wine, gruyère & mushrooms •

coq au vin •

chicken with tomatoes & pimiento •

chicken cannelloni •

carnival chicken with sweet potato mash •

spiced roast chicken •

chicken foie gras •

maple chicken with orange & watercress •

chicken pancakes •

entertaining

chicken galantine

1 To bone the chicken, set it on a board breast-side down. Cut through the skin along the backbone from the neck to the tail. Be careful not to cut the skin from now on. Scrape the flesh away from the bones, gradually working around the carcass, breaking the legs and wings away from the rib cage as you go. Cut off the ends of the wing and leg joints, and pull out the rib cage. Remove the breastbone gently, being very careful not to tear the skin along the breastbone. Using a small knife, scrape the flesh from the leg and wing bones.

2 Spread out the boned bird on a work surface, skin-side down. Fold the legs and wings towards the inside. Trim the bird to a neat rectangular shape. Spread a sheet of greaseproof paper over the flesh and gently flatten with a rolling pin.

3 Mix the sausage-meat and minced veal in a large bowl. Stir in the onion, green peppercorns, lemon rind and juice and sherry. Season with pepper.

4 Spread the mixture over the inside of the chicken and place the tongue on top. Mix the mushrooms, parsley, breadcrumbs and capers. Season and put the mixture over the tongue. Bring up the sides of the skin to enclose the filling and fasten along the top with a skewer. Bring up the ends and sew with a needle and thread to make a neat rectangular shape. Weigh the roll.

2 kg (4 lb) chicken

250 g (8 oz) sausage-meat

250 g (8 oz) minced veal

1 onion, finely chopped

1 tablespoon green peppercorns, drained

grated rind and juice of 1 lemon

2 tablespoons dry sherry

50 g (2 oz) pressed tongue, sliced

50 g (2 oz) mushrooms, finely chopped

4 tablespoons finely chopped parsley

25 g (1 oz) fresh white breadcrumbs

1 tablespoon capers, drained and chopped

25 g (1 oz) butter, melted

1 tablespoon oil

salt and pepper

holly or herb sprigs, to decorate

Serves 8–10

Preparation time: 1 hour

Cooking time: about 2½–2¾ hours

5 Place the roll on a large sheet of foil in a roasting tin. Brush all over with butter and oil, then seal the foil. Bake in a preheated oven, 180°C (350°F), Gas Mark 4, for 30 minutes per 500 g (1 lb).

6 Open the foil, baste and cook for a final 30 minutes until golden brown. To test if the galantine is cooked, insert a skewer – the juices should run clear. Remove from the foil and place on a wire rack to cool. Remove the threads. Slice thinly and decorate with holly or herb sprigs.

chicken suprêmes with roast peppers

1 Roast the peppers under a preheated hot grill, turning frequently, for 15 minutes or until the skins blacken and blister all over. Remove from the grill and place each one immediately in a plastic bag. Tie each bag securely, then leave until the peppers are cold.

2 Unwrap the peppers and, one by one, hold under cold running water and rub off the blackened skins with your fingers. Pull off the stalks, slit open the peppers and remove the cores and seeds. Pat the peppers thoroughly dry with kitchen paper, then cut them lengthways into thin strips with a sharp knife.

3 Heat the oil in a sauté pan, and sauté the chicken over a moderate heat for 7–10 minutes until golden. Remove and set aside on a plate. Add the onion slices to the pan and fry over a gentle heat, stirring frequently, for about 5 minutes or until soft but not coloured. Add the roast pepper strips, the garlic, sun-dried tomatoes, basil and salt and pepper to taste. Stir well to mix, and moisten with wine.

4 Return the chicken to the pan with the juices that have collected on the plate. Cover and cook for 20 minutes or until the chicken is tender when pierced with a fork, turning the chicken over and basting with the cooking liquid occasionally. Season to taste, and serve hot, garnished with basil sprigs.

4 sweet peppers in different colours

3 tablespoons virgin olive oil

4 part-boned chicken breasts, skinned

1 onion, thinly sliced

2 garlic cloves, crushed

50 g (2 oz) sun-dried tomatoes in oil, thinly sliced

2 teaspoons chopped basil

a few tablespoons of dry white wine

salt and pepper

basil sprigs, to garnish

Serves 4

Preparation time: 30 minutes, plus cooling

Cooking time: about 45 minutes

chicken with 40 garlic cloves

1 Wash and dry the chicken cavity, insert the bouquet garni and add salt and pepper to taste. Truss the chicken with string.

2 Heat the oil in a flameproof casserole into which the bird just fits. Add the garlic and celery, then the chicken, and cook until it is lightly browned on all sides. Cover the casserole. Make a paste with the flour and water and seal carefully around the edge.

3 Put the casserole in a preheated oven, 180°C (350°F), Gas Mark 4, and cook for 2¼ hours without opening the oven door during cooking.

4 Break the flour and water seal, then lift out the chicken and place it on a warmed serving platter. Arrange the garlic cloves around the chicken and garnish with sprigs of rosemary, sage and thyme. Serve hot, with mashed potatoes and a juicy vegetable dish such as ratatouille.

2 kg (4 lb) oven-ready, corn-fed chicken, giblets removed

1 bouquet garni

4 tablespoons virgin olive oil

40 garlic cloves, separated but not peeled

1 celery stick, chopped

salt and pepper

a few sprigs each of rosemary, sage and thyme, to garnish

For Sealing:

4 tablespoons plain flour

4 teaspoons water

Serves 4	
Preparation time: 15 minutes	
Cooking time: 2½ hours	

■ Although this Provençal dish contains an enormous quantity of garlic cloves, the end result is not as garlicky as you might expect. The lengthy cooking time enhances the sweetness of the garlic flavour.

chicken & red pesto roulades

1 Make a long horizontal slit through the thickest part of each chicken breast without cutting right through.

2 Beat the butter and pesto in a bowl, then spread the mixture inside the cavities in the chicken breasts, dividing it equally between them. Close the chicken tightly around the pesto mixture. Stretch the bacon rashers with the flat of a large knife blade, then wrap 2 bacon rashers tightly around each chicken breast, overlapping them so that the chicken is completely enclosed in the bacon. Secure with wooden cocktail sticks.

3 Heat the oil in a large sauté pan, add the chicken breasts in a single layer and sauté over a moderate heat for 3 minutes on each side or until the bacon colours. Add the wine and stock and bring to the boil, spooning liquid over the chicken constantly. Cover and simmer gently for about 15 minutes until the chicken is tender when pierced with a fork.

4 Remove the roulades from the pan with a slotted spoon, cover and keep warm. Add the crème fraîche to the pan and boil, stirring, until the liquid has thickened and reduced to a syrupy glaze. Season to taste. Serve hot, with the sauce poured over and around the roulades. Garnish with cherry tomatoes and basil leaves.

6 large boneless, skinless chicken breasts

50 g (2 oz) butter

4 tablespoons red pesto

12 rindless rashers of back bacon

2 tablespoons virgin olive oil

125 ml (4 fl oz) red wine

175 ml (6 fl oz) hot Chicken Stock (see page 9)

4 tablespoons crème fraîche

salt and pepper

To Garnish:
cherry tomatoes
fresh basil leaves

Serves 6

Preparation time: 20 minutes

Cooking time: 20–25 minutes

1 Put the chicken breasts in a single layer in an ovenproof dish, dot with half of the butter, sprinkle with the herbs, and season with salt and pepper. Cover with foil and place in a preheated oven, 180°C (350°F), Gas Mark 4, for 30 minutes or until just tender when pierced with a fork.

2 Meanwhile, melt the remaining butter in a saucepan, add the mushrooms and sauté over a moderate heat, stirring often, for about 5 minutes. Sprinkle in the flour and cook, stirring, for 1–2 minutes. Remove the pan from the heat and add the milk gradually, beating with a whisk. Add the wine in the same way.

3 Return the pan to the heat and bring to the boil, stirring. Lower the heat and simmer, stirring, for about 5 minutes until thickened. Add the cream, two-thirds of the Gruyère, the nutmeg and salt and pepper. Simmer over a gentle heat for 5 minutes. Remove from the heat.

4 When the chicken is tender, remove it from the oven and increase the temperature to high. Tip any juices into the sauce and stir. Pour the sauce over the chicken and sprinkle with the remaining Gruyère. Return to the oven and bake for about 5 minutes. Serve hot, with a crisp salad, if liked.

4 part-boned chicken breasts, skinned

50 g (2 oz) unsalted butter

½ teaspoon dried mixed herbs

½ teaspoon dried tarragon

250 g (8 oz) button mushrooms, thinly sliced

25 g (1 oz) plain flour

300 ml (½ pint) milk

150 ml (¼ pint) dry white wine

75 ml (3 fl oz) double cream

125 g (4 oz) Gruyère cheese, grated

good pinch of freshly grated nutmeg

salt and pepper

Serves 4

Preparation time: 30 minutes

Cooking time: about 35 minutes

chicken with white wine, gruyère & mushrooms

coq au vin

1 Rub the chicken with the dried thyme and pepper. Sauté half the pieces in the oil in a large flameproof casserole for 7–10 minutes until golden. Remove with a slotted spoon and set aside on a plate. Repeat with the remaining chicken. Add the bacon to the casserole and cook over a moderate heat, stirring frequently, until the fat runs. Add the onions, mushrooms and garlic and cook, stirring frequently, for 5 minutes.

2 Gently warm the brandy in a small saucepan. Return the chicken and its juices to the casserole, pour in the brandy and set it alight with a taper. When the flames subside, add the wine and bring to the boil, stirring. Add the bouquet garni and salt and pepper to taste. Cover and simmer over a gentle heat, stirring occasionally, for 40 minutes or until the chicken is tender.

3 Remove the chicken and vegetables to a warmed serving dish with a slotted spoon and keep hot. Discard the bouquet garni. Mix the butter and flour to a paste and add to the sauce a little at a time until evenly blended. Bring to the boil and simmer, stirring, for 2–3 minutes until the sauce thickens. Season to taste.

4 Serve the chicken and vegetables with the sauce spooned over, and garnished with thyme and parsley, if liked.

2 kg (4 lb) oven-ready chicken, giblets removed, cut into 8 pieces

2 teaspoons dried thyme

3 tablespoons rapeseed oil

175 g (6 oz) rindless rashers of smoked streaky bacon, chopped

16 small pickling onions, peeled and blanched

250 g (8 oz) small button mushrooms

3 garlic cloves, crushed

3 tablespoons brandy

350 ml (12 fl oz) red wine

1 bouquet garni

1 tablespoon butter

2 tablespoons plain flour

salt and pepper

To Garnish:

fresh thyme (optional)

fresh parsley (optional)

Serves 4

Preparation time: 30 minutes

Cooking time: about 50 minutes

■ Serve this wonderful dish with a bottle of robust red wine, such as a Burgundy. This is the region in France where the original version of this dish was made famous.

chicken with tomatoes & pimiento

1 Heat the oil in a flameproof casserole, add the onion and garlic and cook gently for 15 minutes. Add the chicken pieces with the pimiento, tomatoes and salt and pepper to taste, and fry, turning, over a moderate heat until evenly browned.

2 Mix the tomato purée with a little lukewarm water, then stir it into the casserole with the wine. Lower the heat, cover and cook gently for 30 minutes.

3 Chop one of the rosemary sprigs and sprinkle it over the chicken. Cook for a further 30 minutes or until the chicken is tender, adding a little more of the stock occasionally to keep it moist.

4 Serve the chicken hot, garnished with the remaining rosemary sprigs.

3–4 tablespoons olive oil

1 small onion, sliced

2 garlic cloves, crushed

1 kg (2 lb) oven-ready chicken, cut into serving pieces

1 small piece canned pimiento, chopped

4 tomatoes

1 tablespoon tomato purée

3–4 tablespoons dry white wine

a few rosemary sprigs

6–8 tablespoons Chicken Stock (see page 9)

salt and pepper

Serves 4

Preparation time: 20–30 minutes

Cooking time: 1½ hours

chicken cannelloni

1 Melt the butter in a saucepan, sprinkle in the flour and stir over a moderate heat for 1–2 minutes. Remove from the heat and add half the milk, a little at a time, beating vigorously after each addition. Return the pan to the heat and bring to the boil, stirring. Lower the heat and simmer, stirring, for about 5 minutes until very thick and smooth. Remove the pan from the heat and transfer half of the sauce to a bowl.

2 Add one-third of the grated Cheddar to the sauce in the bowl with the chicken, sweetcorn, half the nutmeg, and salt and pepper to taste. Stir well.

3 Over a moderate heat, gradually beat the remaining milk into the sauce in the pan. Bring to the boil and simmer, stirring, for 5 minutes until thick and smooth. Add half of the remaining cheese, the remaining nutmeg, and salt and pepper to taste and stir until the cheese melts. Remove the pan from the heat.

4 Pour about one-third of the sauce into a large ovenproof dish and spread evenly. With a teaspoon, fill the cannelloni tubes with the chicken mixture. Place the tubes in a single layer in the dish. Pour over the remaining sauce and sprinkle with the remaining cheese and the paprika. Bake in a preheated oven, 190°C (375°F), Gas Mark 5, for 30–35 minutes until bubbling and golden. Serve hot, with a mixed salad.

50 g (2 oz) butter

50 g (2 oz) plain flour

700 ml (24 fl oz) milk

175 g (6 oz) Cheddar cheese, grated

250 g (8 oz) boneless, skinless cooked chicken, shredded

50 g (2 oz) canned sweetcorn kernels

¼ teaspoon freshly grated nutmeg

12 cannelloni tubes

good pinch of paprika

salt and pepper

Serves 4–6

Preparation time: 30 minutes

Cooking time: 30–35 minutes

4 boneless, skinless chicken breasts

flat leaf parsley sprigs, to garnish

Marinade:

125 ml (4 fl oz) sweet sherry

1 teaspoon Angostura bitters

1 tablespoon light soy sauce

1 tablespoon chopped fresh root ginger

pinch of ground cumin

pinch of ground coriander

1 teaspoon dried mixed herbs

1 small onion, finely chopped

75 ml (3 fl oz) Chicken Stock (see page 9)

Sweet Potato Mash:

2 sweet potatoes

2 tablespoons fromage frais

salt and pepper

Serves 4

Preparation time: 15–20 minutes, plus marinating

Cooking time: about 20 minutes

1 Put the chicken breasts into a non-metallic dish. Mix together all the ingredients for the marinade in a measuring jug then pour the marinade over the chicken, making sure all the pieces are well coated. Cover and leave to marinate in the refrigerator overnight.

2 When you are ready to cook, arrange the chicken breasts on a grill pan and cook them under a preheated moderate grill for about 10 minutes on each side.

3 Meanwhile, boil the sweet potatoes in their skins for 20 minutes until soft. Drain well then peel. Mash the potatoes well and let them dry a bit, then stir in the fromage frais and season with salt and pepper. Slice the chicken breasts and serve with the mash, garnished with the flat leaf parsley.

carnival chicken with sweet potato mash

spiced roast chicken

1 Put the garlic, ginger, chillies and cumin seeds in a food processor or blender with half of the yogurt, the turmeric, mint, mixed spice and ½ teaspoon salt. Blend until all the ingredients are finely ground and evenly mixed into the yogurt – the mixture will be quite runny.

2 Slash the chicken skin through to the flesh with a sharp pointed knife, then truss with string. Put the bird into a large bowl and pour over the yogurt mixture. Cover and leave to marinate for at least 8 hours, turning the chicken from time to time.

3 Put the chicken into an ovenproof dish into which it just fits. Place in a preheated oven, 180°C (350°F), Gas Mark 4, for 2–2¼ hours or until the juices run clear when the thickest part of a thigh is pierced with a fork. Baste frequently and spoon over the remaining yogurt halfway through the roasting time.

4 Remove the bird from the oven, cover tightly with foil and set aside to rest. Keep the cooking juices hot. Discard the trussing string. Put the chicken on a warmed platter and pour over the cooking juices. Garnish the chicken with mint sprigs. Serve with basmati rice and a dish of curried vegetables.

2 garlic cloves, roughly chopped

2.5 cm (1 inch) piece of fresh root ginger, peeled and roughly chopped

1–2 dried red chillies, roughly chopped

1 tablespoon cumin seeds

375 g (12 oz) natural yogurt

2 teaspoons ground turmeric

1 teaspoon dried mint

½ teaspoon ground mixed spice

2 kg (4 lb) oven-ready chicken, giblets removed

salt

mint sprigs, to garnish

Serves 4

Preparation time: 15 minutes, plus marinating

Cooking time: 2–2¼ hours

■ In this Indian-inspired dish, the spiced yogurt forms a dark, crisp crust contrasting with the moist and succulent white meat.

chicken foie gras

1 Heat the oil and butter in a large sauté pan, add the chicken and sauté over a moderate heat for about 5 minutes until golden. Add the peppercorns and salt and pepper, then pour in the wine and water and stir to mix. Cover and simmer gently for 15 minutes until the chicken is tender when pierced with a fork, turning it over and basting occasionally with the cooking liquid.

2 Meanwhile, mash the pâté in a bowl and gradually work in the cream until evenly mixed.

3 Remove the chicken from the pan with a slotted spoon, set aside and keep warm.

4 Increase the heat and boil the cooking liquid for a few minutes until reduced, then add the pâté to the cream mixture and stir until evenly mixed with the liquid in the pan. Allow to bubble and thicken, then taste for seasoning.

5 Serve the chicken with the sauce poured over, garnished with salad leaves.

1 tablespoon rapeseed oil

25 g (1 oz) unsalted butter

6 boneless, skinless chicken breasts

2 tablespoons pink peppercorns, crushed

200 ml (7 fl oz) rosé wine

200 ml (7 fl oz) water

125 g (4 oz) can pâté de foie gras

150 ml (¼ pint) double cream

salt and pepper

salad leaves, to garnish

Serves 6	
Preparation time: 10 minutes	
Cooking time: about 25 minutes	

1 Pierce the chicken legs at regular intervals with a skewer and put them into a shallow dish. Add the orange juice, onion, garlic, nutmeg and salt and pepper to taste. Cover and chill for 8 hours.

2 Lift the chicken legs out of the marinade with a slotted spoon and place flesh-side down under a preheated moderate grill and cook for 15 minutes. Turn them over, brush with maple syrup and cook for a further 15–20 minutes until tender. Test the chicken by piercing the joints in the thickest part with a fork – if the juices run clear, not pink, the chicken is cooked.

3 While the chicken is cooking, make the salad. Grate the rind and squeeze the juice from 1 orange. Remove all the pith and peel from the remaining 3 oranges and divide into segments. Snip the watercress into sprigs. Put the orange segments and watercress into a serving dish and sprinkle with the onion. Mix the orange juice and rind with the oil and chives, and season with salt and pepper. Spoon the dressing over the salad and serve with the chicken.

maple chicken with orange & watercress

4 chicken legs

1 cup unsweetened orange juice

1 onion, thinly sliced

1 garlic clove, crushed

freshly ground nutmeg

4 tablespoons maple syrup

salt and pepper

Salad:

4 thin-skinned oranges

1 bunch of watercress

1 small onion, finely chopped

4 tablespoons olive oil

2 tablespoons chopped chives

Serves 4

Preparation time: 30 minutes, plus chilling

Cooking time: 30–35 minutes

chicken pancakes

1 First make the pancake batter. Sift the flour into a bowl with a pinch of salt. Make a well in the centre and pour in the egg. Add the milk, a little at a time, whisking and drawing in the flour from the sides of the well. Set aside to rest.

2 Meanwhile, melt half of the butter in a saucepan, add the onion and fry gently, stirring, for about 5 minutes or until softened. Add the mushrooms, increase the heat, and fry, stirring frequently, for 5 minutes or until the juices run. Remove from the heat and turn into a bowl. Stir in the chicken, the chopped parsley and season with salt and pepper.

3 To cook the pancakes, whisk 1 tablespoon oil into the batter. Heat about 2 teaspoons oil in a crêpe pan or frying pan until very hot. Pour in a small ladleful of batter, swirl it around the pan and cook for about 1 minute until the pancake is golden brown on the underside. Toss the pancake and cook until golden brown on the other side, then turn out the pancake so that the first side is underneath. Repeat with the remaining batter to make 12 pancakes in total, adding more oil as necessary. As the pancakes are made, stack them up.

4 To make the sauce, melt the remaining butter in a pan, sprinkle in the flour and cook over a moderate heat, stirring, for 1–2 minutes. Remove the pan from the heat and slowly add 450 ml (¾ pint) of the milk, beating after each addition. Return the pan to the heat and bring to the boil, stirring all the time. Lower the heat and simmer, stirring, for about 5 minutes until smooth. Remove the pan from the heat and pour about half the sauce into the chicken mixture. Fold gently to mix then taste for seasoning.

5 Put a good spoonful of filling in the centre of each pancake and roll up into a cigar shape. Stir the remaining milk and the cream into the remaining sauce in the pan and season to taste. Return to the heat and beat until hot.

6 Pour one-third of the sauce into an ovenproof dish and spread evenly. Arrange the filled pancakes in a single layer in the dish and pour over the remaining sauce. Sprinkle with Parmesan. Place in a preheated oven, 190°C (375°F), Gas Mark 5, and cook for 20 minutes until bubbling. Serve hot with a green salad.

50 g (2 oz) butter

1 small onion, very finely chopped

250 g (8 oz) button mushrooms, sliced

250 g (8 oz) boneless, skinless cooked chicken, shredded

3 tablespoons finely chopped parsley

25 g (1 oz) plain flour

600 ml (1 pint) milk

150 ml (¼ pint) double cream

salt and pepper

25 g (1 oz) Parmesan cheese, freshly grated

Pancakes:

125 g (4 oz) plain flour

1 egg, beaten

300 ml (½ pint) milk

3–4 tablespoons rapeseed oil

Serves 4–6	
Preparation time: about 1 hour	
Cooking time: 20 minutes	

index